D1263582

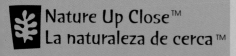

Nature Up Close™
La naturaleza de cerca™

# Corn Up Close
# El maíz

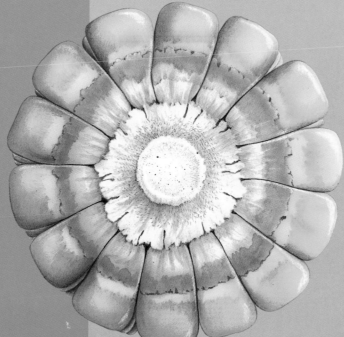

Orange City Public Library
112 Albany Ave. S.E.
Orange City, IA 51041-0346

**Katie Franks**

Traducción al español:
Ma. Pilar Sanz

**PowerKiDS**
press™

**& Editorial Buenas Letras**™
New York

Published in 2008 by The Rosen Publishing Group, Inc.
29 East 21st Street, New York, NY 10010

Copyright © 2008 by The Rosen Publishing Group, Inc.

All rights reserved. No part of this book may be reproduced in any form without permission in writing from the publisher, except by a reviewer.

First Edition

Editor: Jennifer Way
Book Design: Kate Laczynski
Photo Researcher: Nicole Pristash

Photo Credits: Cover, pp. 1, 5, 7, 9, 11, 13, 15, 17, 19, 21, 24 © Studio Stalio; p. 23 Shutterstock.com.

Cataloging Data

Franks, Katie.
  Corn up close-El maíz / Katie Franks; traducción al español María Pilar Sanz — 1st ed.
      p. cm. — (Nature up close–La naturaleza de cerca).
  Includes index.
  ISBN 978-1-4042-7677-2 (library binding)
  1. Corn—Juvenile literature. 2. Spanish-language materials I. Title.

Manufactured in the United States of America

Websites: Due to the changing nature of Internet links, PowerKids Press and Buenas Letras have developed an online list of Web sites related to the subject of this book. This site is updated regularly. Please use this link to access the list: www.powerkidslinks.com/nuc/corn

# Contents

# Contenido

Did you know that corn is a type of tall grass? Corn is an important food all around the world.

---

¿Sabías que el maíz es un tipo de hierba? El maíz es un alimento muy importante en todo el mundo.

This drawing shows the parts of a corn plant. A few of these are the **tassel**, leaves, ears, **stem**, and the **roots**.

---

Esta ilustración muestra algunas de las partes de la planta de maíz. Algunas de éstas son las **espiguillas**, las hojas, la vaina, el **tallo** y la **raíz**.

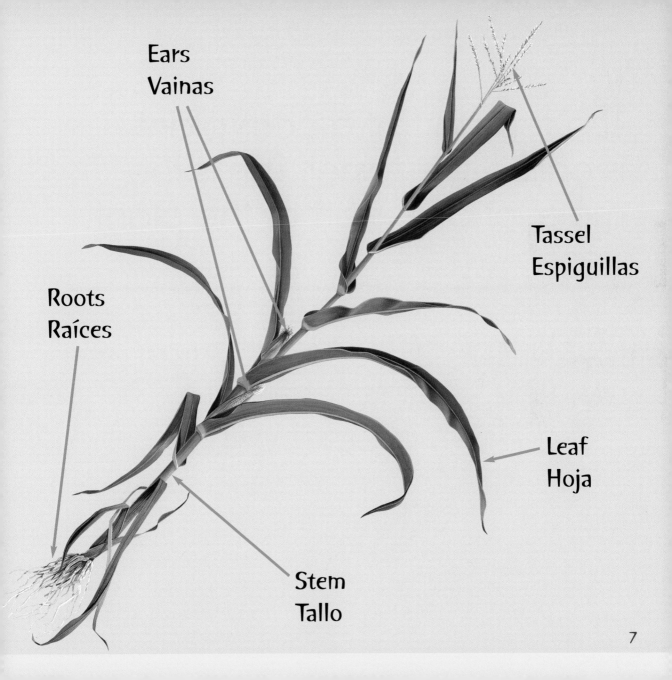

Ears
Vainas

Tassel
Espiguillas

Roots
Raíces

Leaf
Hoja

Stem
Tallo

The top part of a corn plant is called the tassel. This is the male, or boy, part of the plant.

---

La parte superior de una planta de maíz se llama espiguilla. La espiguilla es el órgano masculino de la planta.

9

The ear is the female, or girl, part of the corn plant. The husk covers the ear. The corn **kernels** grow inside the husk.

---

La mazorca es el órgano femenino de la planta. La chala cubre la mazorca. Dentro de la chala crecen los **granos** del maíz.

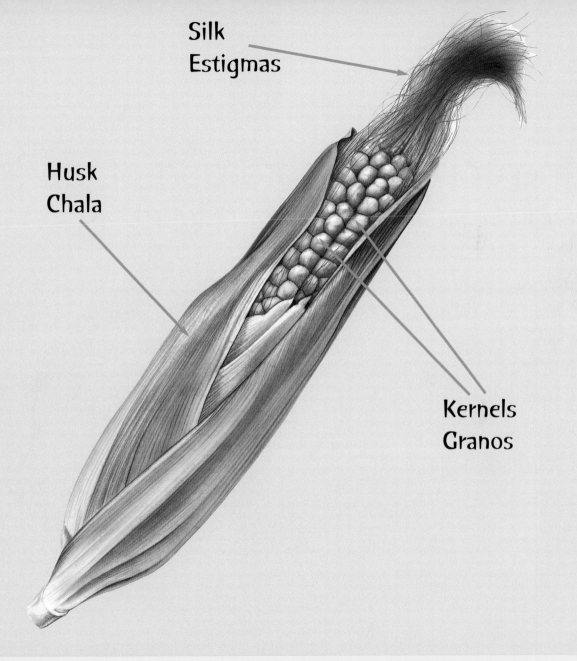

Silk
Estigmas

Husk
Chala

Kernels
Granos

The cob is the hard part of the ear. It holds the corn kernels.

---

La mazorca es la parte dura del maíz. En esta se encuentran los granos.

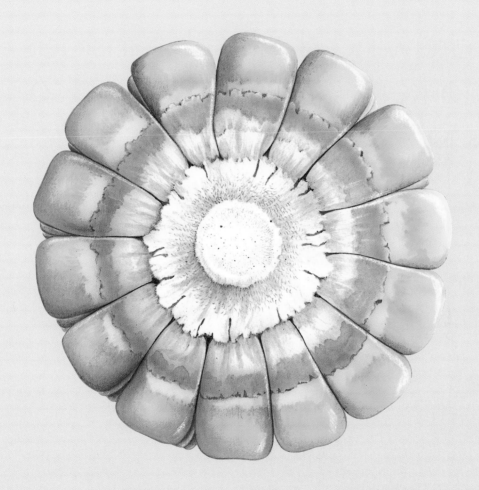

This drawing shows the insides of the kernel. Kernels are also the corn plant's seeds!

---

En esta ilustración puedes ver un grano de maíz por dentro. ¡Los granos son las semillas de la planta de maíz!

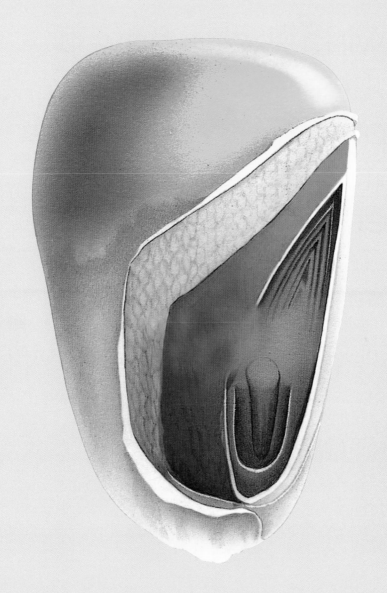

This drawing shows how a kernel of corn grows into a corn plant. The leaves and roots both grow out of this seed.

---

En esta ilustración puedes ver como un grano de maíz se convierte en planta. Las hojas y las raíces crecen de la semilla.

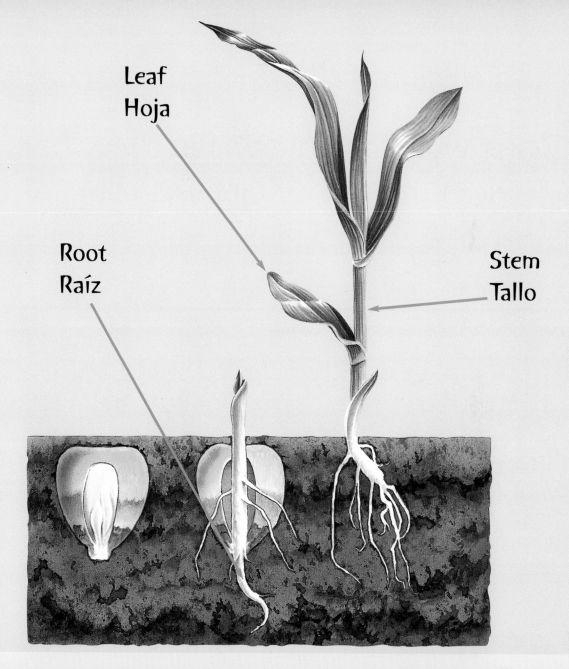

Leaf
Hoja

Root
Raíz

Stem
Tallo

17

Corn was first grown in Mexico. It is now grown all over the world.

---

El maíz se cultivó por primera vez en México. Hoy, el maíz crece en todo el mundo.

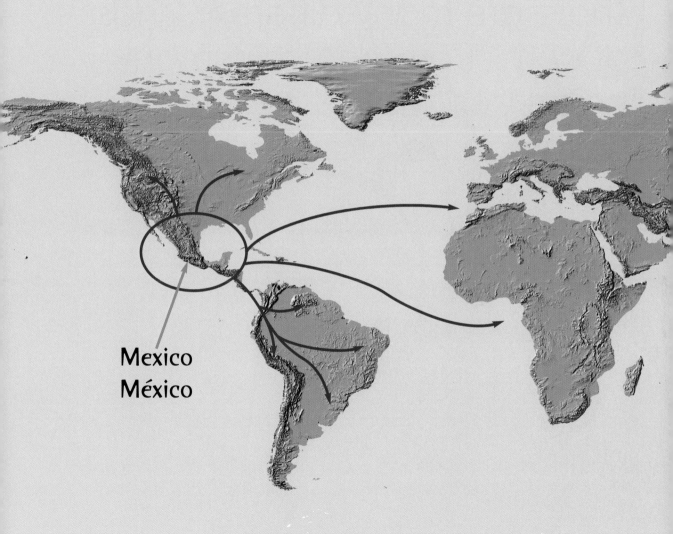

Mexico
México

There are many different kinds of corn. Corn comes in many colors besides white or yellow. Corn can be brown, red, or even blue!

---

Hay muchos tipos de maíz. ¡Además de amarillo o blanco, el maíz puede ser de color marrón, rojo y azul!

Corn has oils and sugars that can be used for many things. Corn is best known for the foods into which it can be made.

---

El maíz tiene aceites y azúcares. Estos se pueden usar para crear muchos alimentos.

# Words to Know / Palabras que debes saber

**kernels**
**(los) granos**

**roots**
**(las) raíces**

**stem**
**(el) tallo**

**tassel**
**(las) espiguillas**

## Index

## Índice